10-9-

The Outdoors Inside Out

Scott,

A Cancer Survival

is Great. Hang in

there. It is about

Attitude. Remember To

Be Grateful.

Love Albert

The Outdoors Inside Out

Tom Hubbard

iUniverse, Inc.
New York Lincoln Shanghai

The Outdoors Inside Out

iUniverse books may be ordered through booksellers or by contacting:

iUniverse
2021 Pine Lake Road, Suite 100
Lincoln, NE 68512
www.iuniverse.com
1-800-Authors (1-800-288-4677)

ISBN-13: 978-0-595-40346-2 (pbk)
ISBN-13: 978-0-595-85609-1 (cloth)
ISBN-13: 978-0-595-84721-1 (ebk)
ISBN-10: 0-595-40346-8 (pbk)
ISBN-10: 0-595-85609-8 (cloth)
ISBN-10: 0-595-84721-8 (ebk)

Printed in the United States of America

Contents

1

TICKS

Have you ever had a tick? I have. Now I am not talking a clock tick as in tick tock. I am talking about a tick. No not a blue tick dog, although a tick can get blue after sucking your blood. The dictionary describes the tick I am talking of, "as a parasite found on animals". The tick I had, found me while I was fishing.

If you have never seen one I will try to describe them. A tick is oval and approximately the size of a ladybug. Picture if you can a flat ladybug with a small toilet plunger for lips, and you have a good idea what they look like. Ticks are bloodsuckers and attach their toilet plunger to your skin and begin to suck your blood to live. It must be this sucking that causes one to itch, for itching is a mild way of describing what went on with me. Usually a tick will attach himself to your leg, or in the hair on your head and you should be grateful for they are easily seen in these areas. My tick was way down under, south of Sydney, Australia. It took me awhile to find it there and after three days of clawing and bear scratching I finally got a mirror out for a look. There in the hair follicles was this tick. I could tell he was planning on staying for he had made a sleeping mat in the underbrush, and was dozing with a smile on his face. My first thought was to pull him off, but after discretly asking some friends they said, "Do not pull on him for if you break his toilet plunger off you could get infection". Try to get him to leave on his own. Sure I thought, I would just sit down and have a serious talk with him. "No, take a lit cigarette and hold it close to him and he will back out because of the heat with his sucker intact." They obviously had forgot where the beast was attached!

Back in the bathroom with cigarette in hand I slowly snuck up on this tick and let him breath the smoke hoping he was allergic to second hand smoke. After what looked like he was enjoying an after dinner cigarette I knew this would not work. I then tried to touch it close to him and missed with me being the only one backing out, as I danced the Fire Curumba.

The next suggestion was to intoxicate him with alcohol, rubbing alcohol to be exact. Hot could describe this brilliant idea and the more I rubbed the drunker the tick became, for it obviously had been awhile since his last drink and he was not backing out on free drinks. The heat to the surrounding area caused me to add a few steps to the dance I was still doing over the cigarette. Finally I decided this tick would have to die of old age. As I sat out on the front porch and after smoking several cigarettes and sniffing the rubbing alcohol I thought of the time when a girl friend of mine came after me with a toilet plunger trying to get my wallet, I decided I had had enough then, like now, so with my mirror in hand I found that tick and removed it once and for all, for I was just that ticked off!

2

MY HUNTING SHACK

I remember the trip home from Ann Arbor veteran's hospital and after three years of continual Chemotherapy, Radiation, and Stem cell transplant I was cancer free. It was on that trip I saw the hand built deer shacks north of Clare, Michigan. I knew I would need one if I were going to hunt deer and stay warm. I had lost sixty-four pounds and weighed one hundred and thirty six pounds soaking wet.

After purchasing my hunting shack I began to work on it throughout the spring and summer. It was slow going for I was very weak, even so painting and insulating went well. The insulation only came in pink panels of Styrofoam and with camouflage curtains and a cheap golden swivel rocker I was almost done. Obvious color coordination was not a concern.

Putting a lock on the door was a problem because the door extended to the corner of my deer shack, and I did not want to bend the lock clasp around corner so I put it on top of the door. I now could just flip the hinged plate up after removing the lock replace the lock into the eye and hunt, and then lock the door when I left and everything would remain secure.

I decided that my chair needed to be adjusted up, and I wanted to put pipe insulation on my windows for a soft shooting rest. As I entered I opened the door and quickly stepped in, tools in hand, I did not give much attention to the slight click as I closed the door and installed my shooting rests on the two foot long six inch high windows. I then jacked up the chair and I thought to myself I'm done. I was ready to leave and for some reason the door seemed stuck, it was then I remembered that little click. I'm done all right; I've locked myself in the hunting shack in my own backyard. Great! Without the lock in the clasp, it latched. Ramming the door with my shoulder did nothing, and I was just about excited by this time. How embarrassing, how will I ever live this down, I thought. I just will not tell anyone, but then one person would not hurt too bad, so I opened the window and softly yelled help, not wanting really to be found this way. The headlines would read: Hunter found starved and frozen in his hunting shack in his own backyard. Get a hold of yourself Tom. It's July! I then decided to rock my troubles away; I was not sucking my thumb! Scratching on the plexi-glass did no good so I tried sliding out the narrow window, but my head almost got stuck, it was too big, not after this I thought. I did manage to see the lock clasp if I could only reach it. I then remembered the long pipe insulation tubes and after ripping one off, I leaned out and was able to unlatch the door. Whew!

I have since spent some good times in my shack, and have taken two bucks from it, while staying warm and cozy the whole time. The toughest job now is watching my portable TV and our football team on Thanksgiving; boy this venison steak sandwich is good. In closing I would like to mention I have been cancer free for over five years. So if you have been diagnosed with Cancer please don't give in, don't give out, and don't give up. There is always hope!

3

COMMON SCENTS AND NONSENSE

Common scents are the biggest problem when it comes to remaining undetected in the deer hunting woods. Human scents from homes, cars and work can send a good buck packing quicker than anything else. With the arrival of spray on scent remover many hunters have disregarded in part a need for clean hunting apparel. Clean hunting clothes are still essential to stay scent free, and important for warmth while hunting.

Clean hunting socks are a must, if your socks stand-alone all by themselves you have waited too long. Scent remover will not soften them and throwing them in dryer could be fatal. I personally have never let a deer smell my feet, but have missed chances at deer because my feet were cold and moving around. Washing does work.

Hunting hats are another problem when it comes to staying scent free. It amazes me that hunters will wear their hats doing backyard mechanics, fishing, to work, and sometimes to bed. One can only imagine the living organism that calls a hat home. Some older hats are even considered lucky, and are worn for years. The only thing I could ever see that was lucky about them is that I did not own it. I have often wondered why bow hunters always wore their hats backwards; I thought it was because the bill would get in the way while drawing their bow. Now I realize that it might have spun on it's own. If your hat rotates on your head and you did not touch it, or there are several sets of small eyes looking back at you from under the brim in the morning mirror it might be time for a new one.

Long underwear should be washed regularly! Many hunters feel that spraying scent killer on the outside of their person is enough, but if you have ever been down wind as they itched and scratched along believe me it is not! One good indication that your long johns need changing is when you spot leg hair growing through the pores of the material. It might be too late at this stage, but you might try hair remover so you can wash them. If your dryer starts to cough don't be too concerned it is just a hairball.

Attracting scents are sometimes used after the descenting process. Apple scent works well in the woods, but if you find yourself killing ants under three layers of clothing or you are being chased by bees you might want to use lesser amounts or at least dilute what you are drinking. Acorn scents work well also, but if you notice the squirrels and chipmunks huddling football style around your stand you may want to cut back on its use.

Last but not least are buck-attracting scents, common sense is important here. Never, never apply Doe scent to your person. Especially the ones called "It's more than love." Some are toxic not only to the bucks, but many a hunter has fallen asleep from the fumes. No one wants to be awakened from a good dream by a buck grunting sweet nothing in his or her ear.

For us who hunt with partners that are less than fresh I sometimes find myself wishing that someone would invent common sense in a nasal spray.

4

NOVEMBER DEER CAMP

Camping out in November is quite an undertaking. The bucks are in the rut and it is cold. Camping in tents in a local swamp far from the road is very productive, and is necessary to get where these big bucks run. If you are willing to go to these extreme measures I have a few suggestions that might help you in your adventure.

First on your camping list should be toilet paper. Not only is it indispensable for its intended use, but also is valuable for starting fires, for runny eyes and blowing your nose from the smoke from the fire you will never be accustom to. Birch bark and oak leaves will work in the place of toilet paper, but it is better to start a fire with them, and save your toilet paper for important times. It is hard to concentrate on hunting if you need to rub yourself on every tree that comes along, like bears we have seen on TV.

Warm layered clothing is a must in the cold woods. I remember warming a foot over our pine stump fire and talking, when my son said, "Dad your foot is on fire." I would not have known for a while for I had three pair of socks on each foot. Casually I pulled one sock off only to find my second sock was flaming also. When I got that one off there was no fire. My fellow campers were having a good laugh, which I ignored. Now having one sock on that foot and three socks on the other my next move was quite obvious, take one sock off the foot where there was three, and put it on the other, now I had two pair on each foot, and was ready to go hunting. Layered clothing works.

Food preparation is important and the clean up. No one wants a food bourn intestinal problem so when we clean our iron skillets we allow them to burn out black in the fire, and then bang the pan hard on a stout tree. This kills everything, and is high in fiber. Running to the stand is one thing, running anywhere else is not good.

Sleeping arrangements are important also, the more people in one tent the warmer it is. It maybe necessary to bring along some shooting ear muffs because the snoring, humming and the occasional calling out in the night for the one they miss the most, usually their wife. It is important that all sleep in the same direction for it is impossible to sleep if your head is at your buddy's feet and he has worn hip boots for three days. Even so having the fellow in the next sleeping bag rub your shoulder in the middle of the night while whispering his girlfriends name is scary, but still it is better to defend your masculinity then, than to die of nasal foot fungus later. Never take a creek bath unless you want your voice to go from base to soprano. Never take your underwear home, burn them and save yourself the money of divorce, just don't burn them at breakfast unless you are low on camp food. Never spit your toothpaste into the fire for the smoke puffs will be the envy of any high cliff smoke signalers, and give away your secret hunting camp.

Camping out with snow on the ground and the cold is tough, not everyone is willing to go this extreme to get a whopper buck, but if your determined and up to things I have mentioned above, do not call me, It's too cold, and I am too old.

5

BOW HUNTING BLACK BEAR

Blood spurted all over the bears face as he sunk his teeth in my leg for the sixth or seventh time. The pain of each succeeding bite had become a distant memory. Screaming and kicking had done little to discourage the bear's attack as I tried to climb higher in the tree that held my stand. Gnashing teeth again found their mark, sinking deep beneath my hip boot and well into the muscles of my calf. The tremendous pulling power of this black bear was awesome. I jerked my leg with all my strength, only to have my hip boot ripped from my foot. The growling and the sound of teeth squeaking against boot rubber added to my fears. The only thing I could think of over and over again was kick! Kick! Kick! Three hundred pounds of black fury again came with teeth clicking towards my now naked ankle. Just as he was about to make his attacking lunge, I kicked him violently. A short silence followed. Would you lay still, that hurt? Every night since you started that darn bear baiting you have been all over the bed! Why did I have to marry a crazy bow hunting bear hunter? "Sorry I said your snoring scares me."

If hunting other species is becoming a little mundane perhaps you should try hunting black bear with a bow. Not only is it a challenge but very exciting. Imagine if you would you are on a stand ten foot off the ground and a big sow bear with a cub comes up to your stand to get a closer look before letting her cubs come in to eat at the bait. Then she gets right up on her rear legs and puts her front paws on your stand, now if this does not raise the hair on your head or fill out your camouflage pants nothing will. Run! Where?

We all have heard the story of two hunters as they walked an old two track headed for their stands when a big black bear rears up in front of them snapping his jaws and growling. One of the guys casually sits down and removes his tennis shoes from his backpack and starts putting them on. The other fellow watches in amazement, and then states, "you will never outrun that bear," the others reply, "The only one I have to outrun is you."

Black bears have two main reasons for aggressive behavior; they are hunger and protection of their cubs. It is commonly known that bear coming to the bait always know the hunter is there, but are just more hungry than afraid. Imagine that you have just walked into a shadowy swamp and you post up in a low stand over your bait. As the evening progresses you hear a bear circling you and knocking down dead falls and snapping their jaws while emitting loud growls. Then when it is too dark to shoot, or see you have to get down and walk out. This will raise your awareness level believe me I know.

My friends wife at a remote hunting camp was having some distress about using the outside bathroom I guess I should not have mentioned the fifty cent piece sized spider I had seen in there. What she did not know was that her awareness of bears was about to increase too. It was with great apprehension that she closed the outhouse door. Quickly I snuck up to the back of the outhouse and scratched on the wall emitting some low growls like a bear. Instantly I heard the charmin holder go into high gear it was going so fast that I imagine it was smoking. I then heard some banging and thumping in the dark interior when finally the door burst open and this lady came out screaming Laarrrry! Larry and I agreed that Joan did not have to be in the woods bow hunting to be aware of black bear.

6

HUNTING ASSESSORIES

I was quite entertained today by all the new hunting accessories on the outdoor channel on satellite TV. There was this new cough sound suppressor that you just hang around your neck on a string, and cough in it. If you do not hear anything you know it worked. I have always coughed into my armpit and that always worked, for anything that comes from this area is unrecognizable, even sound. Besides it is not like I need anything else like a cough silencer to get hooked on a tree step climbing down from my tree stand. The headlines would read, "Hunter found hung from a tree step and no one heard a sound."

The next item was a combination bow or gun sling. Looked like a black rubber band to me, and stretched in all different positions. My first thought was if you hooked that accidentally on something in the woods when it let go you could get to your hunting spot quicker than you expected. One other thing I noticed is that when using it on your bow things could get confusing. Nocking your arrow on your sling instead of your string could produce a pretty limp shot, and besides the last thing I need is another strap on my person to hang up on a tree step as I climb down from my tree stand. The rifle sling could become a repetitive experience. Now getting kicked once when the gun goes off is one thing, but to hold it to your shoulder with elastic? The jackhammer effect could produce the same result as putting all your quarters in the slot at the car wash and not having a firm grip on the spraying wand. Having the gun or bow sling hang up on a tree step could produce a bungi effect with the hunter finding himself back up in his tree stand with the barrel of the gun or a arrow stuck his ear or somewhere that rhymes with ear.

My favorite invention was the hunter's hearing aid. After years of hearing guns going off, and marriage I am sure a few hunters could use one. One what? One hearing aid! Huh? How do you dampen the sound of a gun shot and still hear a frog at a hundred yards expelling abdominal gas under three foot of swamp muck? There must be a switch of some sort on the thing. Much like the hundred-year-old hunter who found a suppository in his ear and found out he had switched something. Aye what did you say? After watching this hearing equipment work even I was sure it would allow me hear yesterdays footprints.

As a practicing nurse (practice being the key word) I could not help but wonder how this hearing device would work instead of a stethoscope on a patient when listening to determine whether the client had active bowel sounds or just needed to be wormed.

These new accessories looked dangerous for me, to be hung, shot; beat to death or stabbed is not my idea of fun. Hunting is a good time, without hearing what is going to happen to me before it does.

7

GRAY MATTER

In this age when marriages rarely last as long as a short land contract it is important that an outdoors person use his head. It is important that the sportsman never gives an impression that his outdoor pursuits are as important than his relationship with his wife or girl friend. How you are going to do this is beyond me. For those that are engaged, having a intelligent lady may seem like good idea in the beginning, but maybe not quite the asset you think it is if you plan too much hunting and fishing later.

An example of too much intelligence: I know a fellow who bought his ninety pound wife a large chrome plated 44 magnum pistol with a scope for Christmas. Now his wife was smart and she knew whom he had really purchased it for. The only thing that saved this outdoors mans life was that she could hardly lift it, the trigger lock, no key, and the ammunition he had hid until later. If your wife is a little heavier than ninety pounds and intelligent you might as well also buy a t-shirt with a bull's eye on it. POW!

No matter how smart your lady is a sure way to turn her head is to start using words like "Cherish". Something like "I cherish these special moments with you."—Phooey. Starting to talk like this just before hunting season is a way to insure you will be allowed to hunt some. If you are half as sincere as you are when grunting in a big buck with your grunt call, you should be all right. If she detects that you are trying to fool her though, you might as well buy that pistol mentioned above and load it. POW!

One guy I know always buys his wife a new dress just before deer hunting season. He always buys it three sizes smaller than she wears. He then explains that he buys it on sale so she cannot return it. He then giggles and says, "She is so busy trying to lose weight to fit into this new dress she does not care about how much hunting I do". This may seem smart, but if he is found out he might as well buy the pistol mentioned above and load it. POW!

White lies are probably not the way to keep a relationship up and running smoothly. Perhaps using the gray matter in your head will work better. If a hunter would only think ahead. For example by counting backwards nine months from the up coming hunting season a fellow can insure uninterrupted hunting season. Now if it does not matter that you will be stuck at home while everyone else is hunting, waiting for his wife to start labor. POW!

Personally I would not like sitting at home studying a dilation chart with a bigger bellied woman that might be as happy as she once was, while waiting for her water to break. I also would be sure my deer rifle was not in reach during her contractions, but if you think about it this would save you from buying the pistol mentioned above. POW!

8

CHILDHOOD

The prerequisite to the outdoors is childhood. How could one not find in my time Cowboys and Indians fascinating? The horses and guns and Native Americans with their bows and arrows, were just naturally a young boys dream. The Indians portrayed back then were really neat. The westerns showed them spiking white men out on anthills, or burying them to their necks in sand, or hanging them up by their feet like a snared animal.

I can barely remember trying to bury my sister by first knocking her down with a dead crayfish only to have the green insides ooze down her face and to have her gag and be gone. I do remember the whipping though.

Hanging the neighbor boy by his foot went better. I explained to him that any real soldier needed to have the experience of this foot hanging so he could become a sergeant someday. After giving him a candy bar and several baseball cards he finally agreed. It took three of us Indians to hang him up by the foot. I do not know who shot me, but when the soldiers attacked we became busy shooting fern stalked arrows at them and forgot the poor hanging fellow for quite sometime. Later as my braves and I pow-wowed to regroup we heard this moaning and only then remembered our captive. Purple would describe our prisoner's head and foot. I do not remember how much I offered him not to tell, but I do remember the spanking.

Learning to throw a spear from a horse was important. So while riding my 24" horse named schwinn I practiced on the neighbors and them on me. Throwing spears of poplar slashings into the bike spokes was a sure way to take a soldier off his horse. One would know immediately if he made a good hit for the wheel would lock up, cleaning out all the spokes and send the rider head first screaming to the ground.

I do not remember how long I raked leaves to pay for bike wheels, but I do remember being grounded in my tee-pee for a month. It always amazed me that as my outdoors skills increased how my punishment did also.

Rock throwing was important for when out of other fighting tools rocks were always available. To be accurate practice was needed and speed for we practiced on ball faced hornet's nests. Pelting a nest was dangerous and stimulating. Stimulating would describe the feeling when I remained too close and a hornet stung me right between the eyes. The swelling began right after the screaming subsided, and by the time I reached home I looked as if I should speak a foreign language. My parents did not punish me for this for I think they were laughing too hard at my appearance.

These outdoor adventures prepared me for the outdoors as well as life. Now when something hits me right between the eyes, or I am buried by burdens or hung out to dry, I just gag, turn purple, and scream!

9

INTERNET WOMEN

As outdoorsmen we should be as careful choosing a wife today as we are picking out a deer rifle or a hunting suit. We think nothing of spending weeks or months deciding on the right one of these, then only to rush right out and get married after a short ten-year engagement. If you are not in a hurry, many men go on line looking for "that perfect women."

When on line it is important that one is not taken in with a twiggy type photo, but on the other hand an aerial photo of the women is not good either unless the land is included. So an up close meeting with your Internet women is a must. You will quickly be able to determine if she too small, too big, or just right. Again take your time. Do not be too impressed by their dominant attributes, one should only be concerned with her biceps. Squeezing her arm muscle will tell you volumes. Too strong means, she could beat you in the marriage struggles of life, too weak means; she will not be good at splitting firewood. Next you should ask her a question like, "How should an outdoorsman treat his wife?" Check your watch. If she goes on over five minutes she is a throw away, five minutes or less is a keeper.

Real skinny girls are good, for thin women are easy on groceries and cheaper to transport; good gas mileage is a plus. A larger girl is good also, for she is warmer in the winter and in general smiling most of the time. I personally like a women that is big boned, heavy framed, for lifting, pulling, and gardening. Make sure she is clean; but one should overlook her having a little engine grease under her fingernails for her ability to change her cars oil is commendable. She should also be able to clean, Clean clothes, clean house, and clean fish. Start her out on northern pike, filleting and removal of the Y-bones. It is important that she is a good looker, no I meant good cooker for if she can cook the fish correctly she is a catch.

Next check her sense of direction, if she knows North from South she will be good at driving deer to you. If she cannot tell you where she is, but knows the way to the casino, she may not be a good bet. In addition if you personally have a need to always to be in good spirits it is important to get a women with distilling experience like Granny on the Beverly hillbillies for this will ensure you are able to over look some of her undesirable traits, for after three or four medicinal gulps who will care.

Now I never said this would be easy, and that is why I am still looking. Perhaps this criterion is just a defense mechanism for continuing to hunt, fish and to have fun, and I guess I will just have to do these outdoor things at great direst, as I laboriously look each night on the computer for that "Perfect women".

10

THE LITTLE THINGS

When things go wrong in the out of doors it is usually a little thing that starts the trouble in the beginning. On my trip to Alaska I stopped in billings Montana for a rest at a friends. John had worked as a police and conservation officer in Alaska for years. He explained how harsh times could be in the wild, and it was important to pay attention to the little things when outdoors. He always told campers not to leave food in camp. On many occasions bear would come in and cause trouble because campers would fail to heed this advice. A little thing like putting the camp food out fifty or a hundred feet would have been all it would have taken to save many lives. Instead he said several times all he would find of the missing campers were their rubber boots with their feet still inside them.

On a lighter note my uncle many years ago was out bass fishing in the moonlight with a jitterbug. In the dark he had hooked up on a bush on shore, a little thing. Now rather than go in and unhook using a flashlight to find his fishing plug he thought he could jerk it loose and he did. The trip to the emergency room and the pain of having a triple hook hooked in his mustache did not seem like a little thing, and neither did the embarrassment when doctor asks how the fishing was.

My personal experience with a little thing happened with No. 2 trap I was using on a trap line years ago. This particular trap was always tripped when I checked and I determined that it needed adjustment so back in the garage as I worked on several of them I came across this one. I could see the pan level was right when I set it on my workbench, but in seconds it snapped shut all by itself. I then determined that the pan tension was too loose and needed tightening. So I then set the trap again by pushing down the springs on both sides and placing the dog in the slot of the pan thus cocking the trap. My screwdriver had rolled to the back of the bench so I quickly leaned over to get it, a little thing when the trap went off springing up and clamping itself on my navel. Now I mean to tell you this was no little thing. The pain followed me all around the garage and when I tried to push the springs for release my stomach gave way. Pulling gave me the appearance of being pregnant and pain had to be close to labor. After several circles in the garage I needed to do something for the pain was getting worse. Finally I ran back to the bench putting my pinched navel up on it, compressed the two springs and freed myself from this foothold trap. Upon examining my stomach I found an orange sized hicky surrounding my navel, looking much like a black eye. Now explaining this to my wife at the time was no little thing.

11

FISHING, A HOBBIE OR ADDICTION?

Fishing is a relaxing time out from our busy world. It allows us some peaceful time in the out of doors. Some fishermen enjoy fishing so much that it is always on their minds. The line between being obsessed with the sport of fishing and a relaxing pastime is a thin one. If you are fishing everyday in practice, or only in your mind you may have a problem. Of course rarely will the infected person admit to having this constant urge to fish. This is called denial; de-nile is not a foreign river with big bass. Denial is the number one symptom of all addictions with the action in this case "fishing".

If your spouse is hinting that three boats, ten fishing poles, four tackle boxes, oars, nets, and the fish finder is interfering in your personal relationships, you are probably hooked and addicted. It is important to note that all addictive persons stockpile, hide, and excuse their need to have a supply of material to support their habit, Fishing equipment.

I once knew a guy who was late for his own wedding because he couldn't get himself home from the lake. Then finally at home only to find his wife unbathed because he had left a thirty-two inch northern pike alive in her bathtub. You would think she would have known what was in her future; perhaps this is a family disease. Fishermen are great at making excuses, and rationalizing. It takes a seasoned chronic Ice fisherman to come up with a reasonable scenario for spending all day on the wind swept ice in below freezing temperatures, when they could be home warm and cuddled on the couch with their loving partner, watching "This old house."

The addictive disease of fishing is usually diagnosed by symptoms, and is readily noticed by others long before the infected person seeks help. A few of the symptoms follow. Owning more fishing poles than underwear, A Canadian passport, Having a bass boat that is faster than your families vehicle, Kissing a fish before release, Your spouse complaining your breath smells fishy, and last but not least, Screaming "NICE FISH in the middle of the night in your sleep. This addiction with fishing could be terminal, especially if you are planning a fishing trip on your next anniversary. Good luck.

12

FISHING PARTNERS

As a fisherman of many years I have been fortunate to have many fishing partners. I would like to tell you that all of them were good, but in fact if I look at the overall picture I find many of them to be less than adequate. A prerequisite to fishing with a person is their ability to fish safely. Even my most dependable partner had his days when I would have to watch him closely. I could usually tell after he knocked my hat off while casting a rubber frog that he was not up to par. The second clue that day was when he dropped a small northern pike on my lap flopping, hooks and all. Lucky for me I could run in a boat.

As in family fishing it is good to know some signs of dangerous behavior so you can avoid some of the pitfalls that are common to the sport of fishing. One the most important rules when anchoring a boat is that the rope is tied to the boat in deep water. The next rule is that you should be sure that it is not wrapped around anything else in the boat before throwing the heavy anchor over board, like your ankle. If it is you may exit the boat prematurely. One partner I nicknamed Ilene for after a couple of ankle stretching incidents I was sure one leg was longer than the other.

There are some rewards to fishing with a partner like some know it all types I have fished with. One particular fellow knew it all, I told him the bank was soft, but he insisted a docking in a specific spot only to step out and sink to his crotch in black muck. Another friend had his artificle plug caught in a bush on shore he insisted on getting it out by himself, so I finally conceded. It was necessary for him to step out of the boat close to shore on a floating log. Now this man was over weight and dressed out at about three hundred pounds. He had no more than stepped out of the boat when the log drifted one way while the boat went the other way. The log rolling antics was quite entertaining with the finale being a butt flop of great proportion. One last partner that enjoyed out catching me, screamed I really got a big one this time as the drag on his reel screamed as the line went out "I'm going to beat you again! Stop the boat". When the boat stopped so did the fish only to find he was wrapped up in my electric motor. He was very quiet as I let him untangle his mess.

In closing some signs of dangerous fishing partners are body piercing in the face, ears, upper lips, fingers and extreme cases the tongue all without having the holes plugged with silver or gold. Having one leg longer than the other, missing fingers with propeller marks in the hand area, or a black eye from a previous fishing trip with another partner.

13

FAMILY FISHING FUN?

If someone suggests you take your family fishing, act as if you did not hear him for they have an ulterior motive. I don't know what you did to them, but it must have been bad. They may even show you a picture of his smiling child, and a happy wife, do not buy into it. I would strongly suggest that perhaps one or both of your friends is an attorney or marriage counselor that is low on clients. Once you clear your friends of these two occupations, and you feel confident in your ability to endure pain, you may decide in a weak moment to take the family fishing.

I believe in being prepared for such occasions, so I will relate my experiences to perhaps save you some discomfort. Do not; do not take anything to drink along for the children unless you have room for a porta-potty. If your fishing motor is low on running hours disregard this advice for it will be broken in when you are through. Do not; do not sit in the middle of the boat when the fishing begins for this is very dangerous. Even when using only single hooks and bobbers it is life threatening at best. My first attempt at teaching my daughter to cast did not go well." Push the button honey, and swing the pole over head and then when the rod tip is pointed to where you want it to go, release the button." She must have heard the part about let go for that is what she did. I watched helplessly as my new pole and reel sank to the bottom in twenty feet of water.

My wife at the time was doing quite well, and like our first date, she out fished me. She also became quite cocky about her abilities, and began to do some creative casting only to have one cast come to screeching halt, ending with the hook stuck in the back of her head. Now the fun had begun, I thought. Do not, do not try to remove the hook at home as the magazines suggest. It is less expensive to go to the emergency room once than counseling forever.

The one joy I did find family fishing was when my sweet little daughter hooked a large bullhead, whiskers and all and swung it into the boat, and dropped it wet and flopping on the stomach of my snoozing sunbathing wife, that was fun. It is important to have personal floatation devices for situations like this.

Seriously, family fishing can be fun, and it is important that your family's first experience is a good one. For those like me who had no success with family fishing I will now just have to sit in the boat and suffer alone, safe, and relaxed.

14

FISHING NETS

Fishing nets are great inventions and many fish that would otherwise get away are caught. The only problem I have with my long handled net is that it works so well I have used for animals it was not intended for.

While on a bass fishing trip a year ago I spotted a pair of snapping turtles that were entangled and fighting or dating I could not tell for sure. They were big and at least fourteen inches across the back and chubby customers. Instinctively I grabbed my net and in a quick scoop they were mine. My father in law is going to eat well on these. My net was so full I could hardly pull them towards the boat. As I moved them they then became aware of me and with the we've been caught look in there eyes they decided to leave, and leave is exactly what they did, right through the nylon bail of my net. Gone in an instant, not unlike a pair of red-faced kids I knew once who were caught in a drive in theater long ago.

The next day found me buying a new bail for my fishing net. Somehow my resolve to use my net only for its proper use eluded me when a friend gave me four hens, (chickens) I really didn't want them but I figured what the heck, I'd bail him out. No pun intended. Bring something to catch them with they are really wild.

Upon my arrival my friend explained that he would normally catch them on their roosts, but because he was leaving immediately we would have to do it now. What you bring, he asked?" My long handled fishing net" That will work. I then went to the end of the chicken pen and chased them towards Bill and as the hens ran by he would reach out and net one. We would then place it in the cage in the back of the pickup truck. As bill netted the last hen I couldn't help admiring his netting skills, and remarked, "You should take up fishing."

After securing the plywood on the cage I placed the trucks spare tire on so the cover would stay on going down the road. The trip home was slow and I was almost there when I heard a bang, immediately I looked into my rearview mirror just in time to see my chickens in mid-air. Quickly I pulled over as the spare tire rolled by. Three chickens headed for the cabins on the lake and one went to the other side of the road. Luckily two of the hens were dazed and I netted them easily, but the third ran under a low deck and was impossible to retrieve. We looked at each other for a while and I could see that you will never catch me look in her eyes, so I gave up. When I stood up there in the windowed door stood a man watching me. I could tell he had some questions about me being in his yard and my fishing net that I didn't want to answer so I left.

The last chicken was really fast, and I chased her up and down between the cabins for a long, long time. At one point a lady came out of her cabin because of the noise and to watch. I came running by in hot pursuit of the screaming chicken with net in hand; all she said was "fishing huh?" Finally I caught her, (the chicken). My face was red more from embarrassment than exertion. The lady was very sympathetic between giggles as I tried to explain.

The first thing I did when I got home was to throw that net back in the boat. Later in the week I saw that remaining chicken cross the road at the same corner. No way I thought. My FISHING net is staying in the boat where it belongs.

15

WHY

Sometimes things are hard to explain. These are a few questions I wish I could answer.

Why is it that before hunting you can use the bathroom 28 times, only to have nature call the minute you enter the woods?

Why is it that a seasoned hunter does not check his swivel rocker in his hunting shack for a yellow jackets nest, before he locks the door?

Why is it that the only time your hunting partner calls you on the walkie-talkie is when there is a big buck close enough to answer it?

Why is it that before you complain to your significant other after a week of hunting camp that no under pants were packed that you did not check your gun case first?

Why is it that we always handle a gun as if it is loaded, only to find out when a trophy buck is close, it is not?

Why is it that a triple hook will hook everything in sight, only to fail you when a big fish bites?

Why is it that just when you get your boat into the perfect position to fish and then have the wind change directions?

Why is it when casting that of all the places for your bait to land, that you hook up on the only Lily pad in sight?

Why is it that a skilled hunter can case a big buck using all his experience, only to have a first time hunter shoot it first in the most unlikely spot imaginable?

Why is it that the first time you trust someone to use your Ice spud that it ends up sticking out of the bottom of the lake?

Why is it that a four wheel drive vehicle will get you into a spot in two wheel drive with no problems, only to find it will not get you out in four wheel drive?

Why is it that a farmer will tell you about all the big bucks in his back field, and let you hunt, but not tell you about the big breeding bull pastured there?

Why would a landowner drive 200 miles to his hunting land that is posted so the deer are not disturbed, sight in his rifle the day before season on the property, and then complain that he did not see any deer?

16

I WILL GO DOWN WITH THE SHIP

Have you ever been out on the lake with a mad man and found out it was you? I have. Several questions come to mind I have asked myself that I would like to share with you.

Why in the first place would a person buy an outboard motor that is seized up unless he was a mechanic? Why I asked myself after spending 143.00 fixing this motor myself, would I have to take it out in twenty foot of water to start it, when it started just fine in a fifty five gallon barrel at home. Why on earth would I not check the drain plug so I would know that it had shrunk after two years of setting so I could stay afloat will pulling my guts out trying to start this special motor? Why is it that a boat that is sinking will not tell you right away? Why would a fisherman be so consumed with starting his motor that he would not notice a lack of movement or the buoyancy in his boat? Why is it that there is not some flashing lights on board giving out a warning, or a voice saying, Danger, Danger, Boat is in the act of sinking. Why is it that he does not pay attention to sounds or his surroundings so he could hear the sounds of running water, especially splashing fountain sounds? Why does he not notice the people watching you on shore while placing chairs like they do for parades? How I asked myself quickly does a man start his motor or row for that matter with one finger stuck in the drain hole of his boat? How could he ever admit that he actually thought of biting the throttle handle while he held it open with his lips? Unless he was having flash back to a time when he bit his sister in-law on the ankle as she swam, if he did not remember how she started running right away. Straight to shore where I needed to go. Why in desperation after choking the motor and hitting it with an oar would he only then decide to row the five hundred water filled to shore?

The next day with a new plan and a drain plug for the boat and spark plugs for the motor I was ready. The drain plug fit perfectly and with new spark plugs I confidently rowed out into two foot of water. Now that I was no longer at risk of drowning or under any pressure or water I was ready to start the motor, and on the first pull it started. Yipeeeeee, coyote! As the motor and I purred off into the distance I could not help humming my favorite song. "There are no white flags above my door, I will go down with the ship, I'm in love,"

17

FIRST ICE

Any good fisherman will tell you that the season's first ice is the best ice fishing. It seems that the fish are filling up with food for the winter. This is treacherous time for the fisherman for he will take chances he would normally not take in his quest for his first few fish. Thin ice and cold water has been the demise of many early ice fishermen.

It is important to know, not guess! that the ice is thick enough to hold you. This is where your fishing partner comes in. It is important that you always have a not too close of a friend, that weighs twice as much as you. Brains are not important. Him having an invisible friend helps, for if you can convince invisible eddy to go out on the ice his buddy will go also. Telling him that if he goes out on the ice first he gets his pick of the holes in your fishing spot, after he drills them. I personally like a guy with a shoe size in a fourteen and boots that weigh in at thirty pounds each. Bob is the perfect name, for that is what he will need to do, "bob" for awhile if he falls through the ice, while I am rigging up my bow and arrow to shoot a life line out to him, for I am not going out there.

Tying a line on your partner and then to the truck is another way to insure ones safety when checking the ice for thickness. This requires a guy that is not as big as the first, for you don't want your vehicle pulled in behind him when he falls through the ice in deep water. I have heard of guys in their insanity, who have even slid a boat out on thin ice to fish and having the ice break as they went, it is apparent to me they were wasting precious fishing time for they could have thrown a plug out back and trolled to their fishing spot. I would think that it would be hard to keep an auger sharp after drilling through so much boat aluminum, because you surely could not get out of the boat and fish. Another way to fish first ice is to plank your way out to where you want to fish. These long boards distribute your weight thus allowing you to fish where you normally should not. It is important that you never get out on the very end of the last board for you can fall through the ice because your weight is not spread over a big enough area. Many people may not know that perhaps surfboarding started this way. Running up hill to keep from drowning creates forward motion with the plank, as a result a sport called, surfing. Where in Hawaii this took place I have not a clue.

Seriously, if you have ever fallen through the ice believe me you will never forget it. It is almost impossible to get out by yourself. There is no guarantee that you will come up in the hole where you fell in. If you don't drown, freeze before you get to shore, die of hypothermia, or have a heart attack you will be very lucky. Thin ice is no joke, it is important that you stay clear of river or creek inlets or outlets for moving water does not freeze as readily as still water. Always be cautious when on the ice for falling in an old spearing hole is possible, and air vent holes can be dangerous too. If you think this will not happen to you think again, it is too late to be cautious when you are under the ice looking up and trying to find the hole you fell through to get a breath of air.

18

GOLDEN YEARS

As older outdoorsmen it is obvious that things are not as they once were.

As people of the woods we need to have a tough exterior but Mother Nature has gone wild with me. We always hear about the golden years when life is enjoyable after we retire, have you looked in the mirror lately? If you are over fifty be grateful that the medicine cabinet is not a full body mirror.

I had taken my hat off for it is hard to bath with it on. I could not believe what had gone on under there since I last looked. Where there was hair before there was none no more, only a few desperate stalks stood straight in the air. As I looked closer I could see what had happened for it must have gotten to hot under my hat and the bulk of hair had moved to my eyebrow area or dove in my ears. One particular hair I had missed on my last shaving expedition stood like an oak between my eyes almost in the center of my forehead. No problem I thought my trusty triple headed shaver will make short work of that. The grinding sound when I attempted to cut it warned me that next time I might need bolt cutters. Perhaps I should put up a garage peg-board for the tools beside the mirror that are now needed. I now looked at my ears and there was a hairball that could block sound waves. Trying to get my triple headed shaver in there was a mind-boggling experience and the noise could cause one to need hearing aids.

Looking over to my other ear, no I did not look through my head, but around the front smarty, I saw my nose, at least it looked like a nose. There on the very tip of it was Felix the nose hair. I named him for we have developed a growing relationship. I have tried everything to kill Felix, paint thinner, pliers, cigarette lighter and he always comes back when you least expect it. I have never been more embarrassed by a hair until Felix. As I cut Felix off I tried to think of the positive side of the situation. I Imagined how he had saved me from banging my head on the closed bathroom door at night for he would act much like a bugs feeler in the dark, but then again sometimes when I would kiss my girl goodnight I was afraid several times that Felix might put her eye out. Below Felix I saw more hair hanging out of my nose all over the place. I could not help but think there was enough hanging out for a mustache. I might add here that one should only use blunt tipped scissors when trying to shape a mustache of nasal hair. This will save on sinus headache medicine.

I then looked lower and saw that the fallen hair had covered my shoulders and chest and I thought I would just vacuum it off, but after taking down the vacuum from the pegboard I found that they were not loose, but actually growing in a new garden spot. It was with mixed emotions that I accepted the situation. Having more than three hairs on my chest was good, but hairy upper arms and shoulders reminded me of a date I once had with a women in Alaska, I thought her voice was way too deep.

This thought stopped me cold and I dared not venture any lower for I could see I had some symptoms of furniture disease, you know, when your chest drops into your draws. I also could see where more equipment would be needed on my pegboard like a hydraulic jack and hedge trimmer, and that was a hair-raising experience I was not up to yet.

19

BOTTOM ENDS

Many people do not realize how much the history of America was shaped by the early outdoorsmen tail ends, rear ends, and bottom ends. These outdoor persons were true to the end. Cabins back then were small and not as big as our yard sheds. Most had low entries to save on heat. It was not uncommon to have to get on all fours to enter much like a doghouse. This might explain the expression "Get your tail end in here."

Imagine riding hundreds of miles on a bucking board in the front of a buckboard covered wagon. One can only imagine after a whole day of looking directly at two horses bottom ends how tiring this can be. Running out of gas with today's vehicles is bad; having your horses out of gas was a good thing. The only other option other than walking was to ride a horse. Many horsemen were bow legged and I assumed that this was from too much riding, and it was. It is important to know that this is not a permanent condition though. For after the rider cooled their bottom end off he could walk straight again.

Riding chaps were developed for this cooling reason. Imagine the increased comfort these outdoors riders could have enjoyed if these chaps had bottoms in them. Why someone did not realize that the build up hot air on a diet of beans would allow the rider a comfortable seat in the saddle, much like air-ride systems in the cabs of semi-trucks today. This would have eliminated saddle sores and be a great rear end relief. On the other hand smoking on this bean diet caused one writer to name his work "blazing saddles".

Many parents conditioned their children and made them obey by tanning their bottom ends thus preparing them for outdoor life. Many a journey across open country ended at the trails end. If you think about it the trail did not just stop. This was not in reference to the "trail," it was in regards to how their bottom ends were doing. Therefore creating the saying, the "end" of the road."

Taking care of your bottom end, tail end, and rear end was important. Blisters, saddle sores and lack of water hampered these outdoor persons travel west. Caster oil was developed to smooth the impact of rough riding, both from the inside and outside. Many can remember when their mom brought out the caster oil how this would get their rear ends up running in many ways.

Many people do not know how the style of dancing was influenced by one tail end condition. Square dancing was for those with moderate pain and high stepping was for those with a burning desire to put the fire out. Now I do not know about you, but my bottom end is getting tired and this is where the tail ends.

20

WHEN THE OUTDOORS COMES INSIDE

We are all accustom as outdoors persons to meeting up with all types of animals and critters in the woods. It is only when the outdoors comes inside that the trouble begins.

As a teenager I can remember moving into a new house because of a change in location of my fathers work. I noticed right off the shed skins from large snakes in the bushes and around the foundation of this house. One day my mother went down into the basement to do laundry when I heard her wildly screaming. I tore down the stairs and into the laundry room. I then saw her pointing close above me, and there over the door was this big snake coiled and in a striking posture hissing his displeasure at our disturbing him. As I looked around there was three more BIG snakes on the half block wall, and all of them were looking angrily in our direction. They were not happy about us disturbing their cool summers retreat. Mom was not happy either and we soon moved. Problem solved.

A few years back I was reading on my side of the bed when I noticed this big hairy-legged spider crawling up my wife's leg. She continued to sleep and I assumed she was too warm and that is why her leg was exposed. The spider continued his advance up her leg, and she twitched slightly and squirmed for his long hairy eight legs were tickling her. I could see by the look in his several pairs of eyes, and the flexing of his fangs that he had something on his mind. As he continued up her thigh I thought if I smash it flat now she would wake up with guts all over her leg and scream. I then thought I would wait a little and maybe he would crawl off of her, so I could kill it. Finally I could wait no longer for this giant spider was in the act of going under the covers with us, so I smashed it. Still my wife remained sleeping. Carefully I wiped the juices and carcass of this dead spider off her leg trying not to wake her, only to hear her say "Can't you leave me alone I am tired". Problem solved.

One night several years ago I was awakened by a blood curdling scream from the adjoining bathroom. Now what? I thought, as I ran in there. "I just sat on a Rat, it is in the toilet stool, "my wife screamed. Sure you did, I thought. I could not help but think she had smelled her own perfume too long. When I looked in the stool sure enough I saw this little rat, trapped because the toilet seat was down, like she harps at me to do. "See that is why I leave the seat up so we do not trap rats," I said. "What are we going to do?" She asked. I then reached out and flushed the toilet. Problem solved.

These types of indoor adventures leave lifelong scars, for when I told her in detail the spider event she has never left anything hanging out from under the covers since, and she always lifts the toilet seat to check things out before using it like I have to. Problem solved.

21

BURNOUT

As outdoorsmen we just naturally spend too much time out hunting and fishing. Spending too much time in a deer bind can have consequences. I had been in my deer blind a long, long time. I had just finished playing the star spangled banner on my grunt call, accentuating the spine tingling parts with my doe in heat bleat. It was then that a big buck came dancing lightly out of the brush. I could tell by the look in his eyes that he had fallen deeply in love with the music maker. I stayed very still, but he spotted me. I could see when he realized he had been fooled, his love turn to rage, like spurned women. He then pawed the ground and came for me with head down. I threw my gun straight into the air in my rush to leave, and ran to the nearest tree, and tried to climb it even though it had no limbs. He was fast and hit me hard, grinding his rack into my chest. It was then I woke up. This could happen to you, we all need to take a break sometimes.

When spearing northern pike in a fish shanty it is easy to become in a trance like state. The hiss of the gas heater and the fumes while looking down an eerie green hole in the ice is quite mesmerizing. The first clue that you are in the burn out mode is when you start talking with your with the spearing decoy. If he answers, you're in trouble. Usually when this happens it is not long before you start to see things. For instance if your see a mermaid swimming around by your minnow this is a clear sign that your need to spend some time at home with the Mrs. One guy stayed so long one day he saw a big black dog swim through his spearing hole, he packed his gear and left immediately. Later much to his relief he found out it was the neighbor shanties dog, a lab, thinking he could retrieve a northern pike.

Even when we know hunting and fishing burnout is possible it sometime comes to light from nowhere. Take for example the hunter who came home from hunting and found that this house had been rented. If that was not bad enough it dawned on him he was not sure the way he took to work. Luckily he found his place of employment only to find he had been fired for missing too much time, he was given three days off for missing too much time, and he had taken a week. Imagine having a stranger answering your door after an extended fishing trip and find he is married to someone very familiar.

In retrospect is hard to maintain balance between work, family and outdoors fun. Rarely will a person be able to earn a living hunting and fishing. Many have tried and find themselves talking with fish, dreaming of deer, and homeless, which is not normal. Spending time with ones family, and showing up for work is normal. Normal is also a setting on your clothes dryer, Oh what fun!

22

OUTDOORS WOMEN

We all know the female sports enthusiast have harder time getting outdoors. Many people probably do not realize the primary factor in the invention of the baby bottle was so mom could hunt and fish. How could an avid she-hunter expect to shoot a big buck or reel in a big bass and breast feed her little Daniel Boone at the same time? The father could not do it in most cases, thus the invention of the baby bottle.

Many single women know how to lure a fellow into range, so why not use your insights while hunting. Wearing the right perfume and switching from your favorite one named; "Make Him Your SLAVE" to Molasses with a touch of apple juice thrown in, will work.

Next get into your trim fitting silk camouflage suit, and wear your ear corn earrings with your apple red lipstick. Now if does not lure in a big buck in the woods, it might work down town.

You must be aware that if you walk into the woods like this the animals might start doing crazy things. If a squirrel comes up and starts doing gymnastics on your bowstring, just ask him to marry you. I will guarantee all you will see is his bushy tail as he leaves. This works in the woods and down town on the squirrels as well.

For those women who already have their oval mouthed minnow hooked, keeping your man content while you are out hunting is the main reason they invented the pacifier. Handing these out to all twelve children will work on the noise, but be sure to save the biggest pacifier for your man, a small boot will work for he is accustom to having his big foot is his mouth most of the time.

It is important that you never take your boy friend or husband out hunting with you for he will not be of any use in the deer blind, and he is worthless at figuring out a grocery list, hair appointments, and has no idea on the your favorite soap. "As the world swirls," and he surely does not have a clue if Mary should leave Wendell because he will not leave her alone, so she can go fishing.

Why should smart fisherwomen have to take time out from fishing to wash clothes, cook, and change those hooey diapers? If she would only think about it she could get out of all these chores by simply leaving the breakdown of the child support payments from the friend of everyone but him, on his night stand. Not only will this relieve you of all these duties immediately, and I will guarantee you will get a full night of sleep tonight for a change.

In closing I feel that I should warn you girls not to use all these suggestions at once. If your man never takes out the garbage or supports your outdoor activities, how could you expect to receive a check from him in the mail? Remember if you leave him to long alone, and he gets to the point that he is disgruntled with changing diapers, (No pun intended) you might find you are the one receiving a pacifier in the form of the boot.

23

NO FLEAS PLEASE

Sitting in my blind tonight I could not help but think of the part that fleas play in our lives. I have never read an outdoor article on fleas, but personally I think fleas have played a big part in our interaction with our hunting dogs and pets in general.

Fleas date back to early times and in medieval times most aristocrats had two castles so when one got flea infested they could move to the other. If you have ever had a flea problem in your home you know exactly what I mean. One year our dogs had fleas real bad in spite of our efforts. I finally asked my wife to go to the veterinarian for help. He said after checking our dog Jack, that the fleas would be bad until the snow flies. My wife looked confused and then said, "Snow flies when do they hatch?" No the Vet said, you know when it gets cold and the snow falls from the sky? Still she continued, puzzled, "I did not know snow flies ate fleas". The kids continued to tug on their step-mother and finally to their relief got her to leave. Fleas will do that to you.

A good indication your dog has fleas is when instead of hiding when you run his bath water that he stands up and barks, Pick me, Pick Me! History is full of consequences caused by fleas. Henry the eighth may not of had a problem with his wives; he just might have stayed too long in castles infested with fleas. Nero might not have been crazy when he burned down his house and Rome he probably was just trying to rid his house of fleas. Saloon dancers in our old west probably were decent people if the truth were known they were just trying to rid themselves of fleas in their bloomers and petticoats. Why else would you throw your legs so high the air? Fleas!

Our hunting dogs were good hunters, but they always had fleas. I do not know if there was an effective way back then to rid our dogs of them. All we had was flea powder. I do know as kids we would sneak up behind the dog box of a sleeping dog and smack it hard with a base-ball bat and that a few fleas were left behind when the dog went ballis-tic, and when the dog hit the end of the chain a few fleas were displaced by the dogs sudden stop.

Many old time cures were more painful than having fleas. One of these cures was that you personally would shave one side of your head, light fire to the other side and stab the fleas with an ice pick when they came into the open. Not only would this simulate your skin, it would increase circulation; thatch your hair and air-ate you scalp.

We once had a big male bird dog we occasionally tied to a dog box. Now I just thought he was a pervert because he would drag his dog box all over the neighborhood to meet girls, and in this incident he dated a wirehaired terrier, when the puppies were born they had long spider like legs, short bodies and resembled giant fleas. Now that I look back I wonder if his dog box was infested with fleas and he was just trying to get away. The last I knew Mr. Edwards never gave all those puppies away, and I am sure he would say no more fleas please, and probably not nicely.

24

TWO HUNDRED YEARS

I was thinking the other day that I was born two hundred years too late. The longer I thought about it the more I knew I was crazy. The lack of modern conveniences made me think again. Two hundred years ago old family remedies were common-place for there were few doctors.

Imagine having a tooth pulled by the barber with no pain-killer, as others sat around watching the fun. One outdoorsman I heard about treated a wound on his leg with a salve made of axle grease and spider webs. Another remedy that was used in olden times was snakeroot. This Native-American medicine was used for everything from arthritis to indigestion. On this particular occasion an Indian lady was treating my old neighbor, and he purchased some for general ailments. Now I would have questioned this particular fellows reliabilities before I drank any of his tea, for he was the outdoors man who filed his lower teeth down level with a horse rasp to better hold his snuff. Even so three neighbors brewed up a batch and drank it. Soon after a questionable dose they all quickly forgot their original problems for fear of dying. It was obvious to me that they might, for they all lay slumped around with their tongues almost hanging out mumbling what sounded like, water, water.

I then wondered to myself how years ago the outdoorsmen checked their cholesterol. They obviously gauged it by the number of servings of salt pork or the number of eggs they cooked in possum fat. Just the sound of this gives me chest pains.

Bath rooming was another delight. Outside toilets were cold in the winter, hot and aromatic in the summer. There was no double quilted toilet paper back then unless you were to use several pages of the catalogue you were reading. Rough on outdoors persons.

Makeup for the woodsy women was scarce and cornstarch and pinching ones cheeks to make them pink was the best they could do. Rendered lard was used to soften skin, smelled real good too, and gave her an attractive shine. How else can we explain families with as many as nineteen children?

Bathing was seldom, and when a person would get powerful gamey there was two choices, go down to creek, or haul and heat bath water. Persons who bathed too much were considered fiends for most thought baths weaken ones constitution. I would think being too close to one of these old outdoorsmen would weaken mine.

Clothes of animal skins must have been uncomfortable. Stiff when dry, soggy and heavy when wet, and an aromatic delight in the sun. Imagine, no bath in a week, in clothes not the best smelling new off the animal, and plowing in the sun all day, and then trying to clean up in a small dishpan of water for supper. Sha-zam!

Today I know my cholesterol is good, my daily bath will be warm, my clothes are drying in the dryer and when I am done reading in the bathroom, I will not be flushing any pages down the toilet. The only thing I will flush today as an outdoorsman is the Idea of wanting to live two hundred years ago.

25

NIGHT CRAWLER HUNTING

Night crawler hunting? What's that? Night crawlers are large worms and are used for fishing bait. Without becoming scientific, these large worms come out after dark in the rain for air, because of saturated soil, and you will find them stretched out in the grass. People are often surprised that they have thousands in their yards. Without asking permission the owners can become quite hostile when they find you in their yards after midnight. Somehow it is hard for them to understand why anybody would be out with a flashlight looking for giant worms in the rain. For those of us whom do this regularly we also find it hard to give a plausible explanation?

Most inquiring minds can accept our motives when it comes to gathering bait, but really find it hard to justify when considering the time of night, and the weather conditions. As a teenager I once asked the father of a girl I liked if I could take her out night crawler hunting. I only asked once for he would have none of it. I think he misunderstood, maybe he thought I was taking her out in the night and hunting for a place to crawl around. I don't know. Maybe he was right.

Night crawler hunting is great fun and will save an avid fisherman many dollars on bait. The pre-packaged night crawlers seem quite docile and slow compared to the ones captured by hand, maybe because they are refrigerated. What I do know is that the night crawlers in the wild are fast. Locating a night crawler is easy for all you do is quietly sneak around with flashlight in hand until you spot one of them. They are easy to see for they will glisten in your light, because of the rain, and the slime that covers them.

Now that you have zeroed in on your night crawler you slowly creep up, carefully, not too much light for they are sensitive to it, and then quickly grabbing it around the neck before they can retract down their hole, much like a child sucking a piece of spaghetti in. Slowly, you then put upward pressure and withdraw it from its hole. Success! It might be important to know that night crawlers don't have heads in a normal sense, with eyes. They only have a thickener end, so behind this is a collar, their neck, I guess.

Imagine if you would a whole can of fifty writhing, wiggly, slimy night crawlers and you get the picture of a night well spent. If you are ever fortunate enough to be asked to go night crawler hunting, go it is fun, really. I bet for sure it will make a memory you'll never forget.

When asking anyone that has went night crawler hunting, I am answered first with a smile, and then the rest of the experience.

26

CONFUSED

It seems in today's world with events happening so quickly it is easy to become confused. After a full week at work we are usually ready for the weekend so we can relax. Many of us let our hair down each weekend if we have not pulled it out for some reason along the way. The outdoors person uses hunting and fishing for this very reason, to relax. It is important that we not take our work ethic out in the woods and make that also a stressful situation. That is why it is all right to be in La La land or confused part of the time.

Let us take for example the fellow who shows up at his hunting blind with his fishing pole instead of his deer rifle. Now this guy is confused. He should not get overly upset for if he were that worn out he probably would have fallen asleep of exhaustion anyway.

Another sign of confusion is when fishing you find you keep rowing in circles with your fishing boat, forgetting one of your oars is usually the reason for this. It is easy to become confused, but realize you only forgot and try not to be confused, just lengthen your single rowing stroke, and lean the way you would like to go. You will eventually get where you want to go around midnight, and are probably too tired to fish and find it is a good time to take a nap.

Many outdoors persons get confusion mixed up with forgetfulness. A good example of someone who has this idea straight is the women who got to her vacation spot and realized she had forgotten her husband. Now this is forgetting in the truest form. Two days later when out fishing with her handsome male guide her husband shows up, now this is a classic example of being in La La land with a little confusion thrown in.

My personal experience happened in nursing school. As a student medication was only to be given with an instructor present. This particular patient needed a suppository for constipation. Now with glove on hand and I thought my trusty instructor by my side I proceeded with success, only to find my instructor had left sometime during the procedure. Now I was sure everything would come out all right in both situations, but found myself in the head nurses office of the school three days later. For I was being written up for passing a medication without my instructor being present. I tried to explain as a hunter I always noticed movement and the instructor was there. Now I recognized that this old nurse was in La La land as she brought the write up around the desk to me and that she also needed medication, for she was full of it, confusion. I was tired of trying to explain and just quietly signed the write up stating for a reason in the place provided that I was "CONFUSED!"

27

FLYFISHING

If you are ever asked to go out fishing with a guy with a new fly rod I have one suggestion, forget it! I made that mistake once. I left shore as a sane human being only to return a complete wreck. The fellow I went with was a southpaw you know left-handed. Paw would describe what I needed to do to survive. We were using rubber spiders for blue gills, the spiders were cute to look at, but when they go by at 100 hundred miles an hour things can get pretty scary.

Now this particular fellow had the water beat literally to death with his line and the spider, and I imagined a floating roto-tiller could not have made any more froth and waves near the boat. To complicate things further he began throwing equipment over board. First he hooked his other fishing pole and threw it in. Next an oar went by. Finally he hooked his self in the rear end pulling up his pants, which finally covered the sight that was also destroying the fishing and my view. I was sure if he continued to yank on the line he would cause himself a snuggy with his underwear pulled tight. When the hook finally hit home he yelled and the pulling stopped, and he explained he could not control this light little rubber spider, and he thought heavier bait would help his fishing technique.

I could not believe the size of the popper he pulled out and put on his fly leader. I had just got use to dodging, like a lightweight boxer now I had graduated to heavy weight class with a knock out very probable with this big popper. A popper is correctly named for that is the sound made when he hit himself in the forehead. When the staggering stopped I thought he would put it away. I tried to explain nicely that the object here was to drop the fly or popper lightly so it would look like it had landed not crashed, and that the fish were probably afraid like I was of getting hit.

A little later he asked me if I thought the boat was drifting I reminded him that earlier he had repositioned the anchor with a previous cast and it would be all right. Now I had had about enough of this for my fingernails were gone, my eyes were twitching, but still intact, and I was out of breath for I was not use to going ten rounds. Finally his back cast ended with me having fly line wrapped around my neck and with me expecting to take a fast trip, I said quickly, "Take me home, I have to go to the bathroom." I never told him that I already had!

28

THE LAUGHING TREE
FROG

A few years ago while hunting one of my favorite spots I saw a big ten-point buck, and for several nights he would always come out at dark across the field from me. This forced me to move my tree stand, and on this particular night I showed up early so I could get hidden high in the early fall leaves. I had just pulled my bow up when the deer began to come out and feed. Suddenly all the deer spooked and disappeared. I could not figure out what happened for I was down wind, and I knew they had not seen me. It was only a few minutes when I saw the problem, someone was moving in the woods across the field from me. Great

I thought, another trespasser. Slowly in Indian fashion this fellow snuck along. Eventually he worked his way in my direction, and finally came right up under my tree. Now this guy was on a mission so I let him continue with his hunt. I stayed very still for in spite of my disgust I was intrigued with this guys antics. I could not help but notice his lack of camouflage clothing and the shine of his bow blinded me several times, a beginner I thought.

Five minutes had passed and all this fellow was doing was studying the ground and looking into the woods. I finally was done, for this guy was ruining my hunting, if he hadn't already. Why I did what I did next I'll never know, probably disgust, so in a low voice I quietly went Ribit! Now this got his attention, even he knew this was too loud for a frog, and I could see he was trying to think this into the category of hearing things, so I waited. When He had convinced himself he was hearing things he then went into the woods behind my tree and picked up a stump and placed under my tree for a seat. Now this was too much for me so when he became occupied again with building of his make shift blind I again softly murmured another, Ribit! Now he knew he had heard right, and he looked pretty perplexed. This reaction was more than I could stand for I was doing all I could to hang on up that tree as I tried to suppress my spasms of laughter. Some how I gained control of myself, and I could see this poor fellow was getting pretty nervous with his new outdoor experience, and I think out of confusion he just sat down. I also could take no more of this fun so when the final Ribit came out my mouth he tilted his head back he saw me above him, and with an expression of relief he stated half embarrassed," Sorry, I guess you are hunting here." "No I stated." I was just leaving."

29

FLYING BOATS

The big truck with the boat and trailer came off the boat ramp right in front of me. Water came pouring out the drain plug-hole spraying the road and my newly washed car. As I followed along I could see what looked like sparks mixed in the water drops and when the fellow turned I could see he had forgot to hook up his safety chains. Sparks flew in all directions, and I quickly backed off of him a fair distance.

Have you ever had a day when you knew right away to beware? Well this was one of them. It started right after my morning shower, trying to put my foot into my leg hole in my underwear started with me missing it, and with me having to hop around with my foot hanging out the fly. Now I mean to tell you this will scare people, and when all the screaming stopped I was able to get my foot in the leg hole. I knew right then to watch out.

Watch out is what I needed to do when the lights flashed on the boat trailer. First both blinked then one and then the other then one went out and the other brightened up. I knew this was some kind of warning, but was not sure what it meant. Finally we were able to get up some speed with me a long ways back when I noticed a waving in the boat and trailer. Finally the trailer, boat and motor left the towing position and decided to pass the truck and violently jerked to the left. The truck driver must have seen it for he hit the brakes and the fishing boat and all went by. I could see the owner eyes get big when he realized what had happened. I thought I heard swearing, but I am not sure for by then I was lagging way behind.

Now this boat was doing very well on it's own I thought, but the on coming traffic had other ideas for they were running into the ditch and wildly swerving around when finally the boat come back into it's own lane then into the ditch and flipped over to a stop, exhausted. The outboard motor now looked like an inboard for it was in the center of the boat and the fourteen-foot boat snubbed nosed was now was shorter than twelve foot.

Finally when all the excitement was over I tried to console the boat owner. All he could say was, "I knew I should have stayed home when I got my foot caught in my underwear this morning."

30

MOSQUITOES

The mosquito with their gentle whine in the night that keeps you awake by landing and trying to suck your blood we all can relate to. It usually takes awhile but eventually they will drive a person to slap until you kill them or beat yourself half to death. Many domestic violence calls might stem from this scenario, by missing the mosquito and slugging your sleeping partner.

We were on a lake that was infested with mosquitoes and I had used the entire can mosquito repellant and was still slapping myself silly when I asked my fishing buddy how he was doing with them and their torment. All he said was," Just have to ignore them." When I turned around I could see blood and dead carcasses all over his face. Looked like he was ignoring them too.

Now if you really enjoy fighting with Mosquitoes fish in Canada, not only do the deer dress out over three hundred pounds, but the mosquitoes are not far behind. I had just laid down after a hard day of fishing when that familiar whining sound began. I had sprayed the fifth wheel trailer earlier and I reeked of mosquito dope from applying it during the day. They will not bother me. It was just about then that one dove into my ear. Ya Hoo and the slapping and digging began; finally I smashed him with my ear ringing like a dinner bell for the aerial attack had only begun.

I then covered up in the sleeping bag, but at eighty degrees I could not stay in there long so when I came out for air the attack resumed. I had had enough so I jumped out of bed turned the light on with killing on my mind. I could see over by the repellant can a flock of mosquitoes hanging around it, and one sucking the juice from the spray tip. There behind the aerosol can lay a mosquito leaning on her elbow. I could see through her flight glasses that her eyes were blood shot. Beside her lay her partner in crime with a crooked mouthpiece or soft elongated mouthpiece as described in the Webster dictionary. Webster goes on to say that only females bite and suck blood. Obviously the mosquitoes were not the only ones buzzed up right now.

Now I once had a girl friend with an elongated mouthpiece and she would bite, but she saved me many steps for she could kiss me goodbye from across the room. Felix the nose hair liked her too for they would sword fight often. Finally I came out of the repellant induced dream and threw the can of mosquito dope out the door and to my amazement the mosquitoes left with it. Much like that girl friend that also left with the dope when I threw her can out.

31

MIDAIR

Have you ever noticed how some outdoorsmen have their feet planted firmly in mid-air. I have had several experiences with this problem. Borrowing my brother in laws home made tree stand was not a good idea. The climbing stand worked well and I immediately put my seat belt on when I reached the desired height. I settled in and was off in a hunting daze when this stand dropped out from under me leaving me swimming at sixteen feet above the ground. Running in mid-air could describe some of my acrobatic feats and swimming covered the rest of my reactions. Later the stands owner told me that this particular tree stand did not work in popular trees.

Practice is always essential for partridge hunting because these birds are fast. Partridge on take off have a way of banking to the left or right to invariably put a tree between themselves and the shooter to keep from getting shot. Now one would think walking with both feet firmly on the ground a hunter would be safe from the mid-air syndrome. The hunt was going smoothly until I felt a wiggling under my left foot. Startled I looked down and I could see I had stepped on a big green snake. Back in mid-air again, running.

Hunting with a bow is always a challenge. Now with years of experience and too much cancer treatment I am unsteady in a tree stand so many times I prefer to hunt on the ground. I was surprised when the ornery old landowner with a smile let me hunt his whitetail deer infested back pasture. The next morning found me sneaking across the fence just at daylight. I was almost to my blind when I heard this grunting sound close behind. The breeding bull came a full speed and with no hate in his eyes, for he had never seen a camouflaged cow I guess, and he was real excited, LOVE. So was I, excited. Now this big boy was gaining and I decided run, might be a good idea, as I ran I could see my only chance to escape was to get over the fence, and in a short time I reached it. I could feel the big bulls hot breath close behind so I dove over it. Now I am here to tell you that I was never so glad to be back in mid-air again.

32

BIG FISH

Now that it is summer it is important that when swimming you forget
the pictures of the monster fish you saw in paper caught by ice fishermen last winter. Try not to remember the snarling teeth that hung out
of their mouths like alligators. It is also important to remember there is
no record of northern pike attacking or biting a swimmer. When
swimming in weedy area it is probable that you can get tangled up in
them but realize immediately that this is normal and not a biting fish.

Many people do not know that some sun tan lotion has attractive
properties not only for the opposite sex, and are sometimes made of
oils from fish. It is probably best if one does not tempt nature. Catching a big fish with your body in a bathing suit by smelling vaguely

familiar to a predator like a northern might not be as fun as it sounds. It is important that you check out your tanning solution so you are not wearing essence of a shiner or sucker minnow into the water. Save that lotion for the beach only.

For many of us who spend many hours on the lake fishing each year it is not uncommon to a see baby duck disappear from the surface of the lake, grabbed and eaten by the northern pike. This is perhaps the reason most mermaids do not splash around on the surface and never wear tanning oil. For those slow mermaids they also learn in time it is not attractive to have notches taken from their tails by tantalizing the pike.

Now the story above is very close to what I told my sister in law when I took the family swimming. The lake we were going to had a history of big fish being caught with some northern pike weighing upward to twenty pounds. Imagine having one grab your arm to the elbow, I told her.

I had brought along my snorkel and fins and mask, and it was easy for me to go long distances under water with them. Somehow I came up with the idea it would be fun to scare my sister-in-law while she swam. Diving deep I paddled my way to her ankle and turned my head like a shark and bit her lightly on the ankle. Now the explosion happened immediately with her running several miles on my head. I could hear the screaming under three foot of water, and she looked like a boat motor going to shore with a very big wake. I do not recommend this for I almost drowned between by being stomped to death and laughing. So if you feel something like a bite in the water swimming this summer do not be fooled for it is probably just a weed or worst case scenario your brother in law.

33

STUCK

If you spend any time in the outdoors no matter how proficient you are you will eventually end up stuck. It is amazing how one can get into a spot in two-wheel drive but are not able to get out in four-wheel drive. Many of us who spend time down old two tracks know how it feels to be stuck with no one around to help. Invisible Eddy is no help no matter how loud you scream and yell at him.

Now I thought I found a device that would prevent me from ever getting stuck again. It was called, "come along." This device had a ratchet handle and a cable with a hook to suck your vehicle out of anywhere. Two tons vertical lift. Now I was stuck in the muck pretty deep and could not move, so out came the come along. I then hooked one end of the cable to a tree and the other end to my truck. I was ratcheting away, but the truck was not moving. I again ratcheted only to see the tree moving towards me. Wrecker time.

Sooner or later an outdoorsman will need someone to pull him out. I would recommend it not be your spouse. In fact a good way to end a relationship is to pull your wife or girl friend, or to have them pull you. Somehow the communication gap that already exists is accentuated when one is stuck.

A girl friend of mine tried to pull me out one early morning for I had put my car in her ditch because of snow snake venom. This venom is commonly found in the winter and usually comes in a six-pack. I mentioned casually "ease me out" for my old cars bumper was weak. I then heard the engine screaming and felt a violent jerk, and then a clanging sound like metal on the pavement. I had not moved an inch so I got out and walked around back for a look. When I looked at the rear end of my car I could almost see the back of the engine. Gone was the bumper, taillights and filler tube for the gas tank.

Why is it that no one can get the concept that when pulling another with a tow chain or strap that the car in the rear should do the breaking when you come to a corner and need to stop? This slows both cars and prevents smashing the front car in the rear if the front car needs to stop. Now I thought we had this part clear so when I came to the stop sign I waited as long as I could for her slow us to a stop, which never happened so I hit the brake in desperation Wham!

Now the book I was writing was not a romance novel, it was called: Dentures on the dash, by I spit when the cars hit!

34

MEMORIES

If hunting and fishing always ended with a big buck or a limit in fish, the woods would desolate and the waters empty. If these sports were always productive what would be the challenge?

Expecting to be successful is fine, but feeling too discouraged because we saw no deer or we did not get a bite while fishing, we might be over the line. Perhaps we are missing the point, by not realizing that planning and participating is the real fun.

If I think back as I sit here in my blind, the things that stand out are the memories. I still remember my two year old sons first fish, a three inch perch, and how cute he looked holding it in his little suspendered suit, and how happy he was. How could I forget the deer hunting trips with my dad, as a new hunter and cold, how my dad would start a fire to warm me using birch bark to start an old pine stump and how we all sat around and had lunch later. Of course we were all after a big buck, but the wise ones around the fire were just enjoying the moment. For those who no longer have this opportunity for their partners are either too old or have went to their reward, I am sure they would not trade those precious memories for anything.

The sit down stories of days of old and the hunting spots we named, like fire island, the old mans point, eight point ridge, and the north and south beaver dams. Who could not wipe a tear as the bird hunter talks of his memories of his faithful pointer who has long went to his reward?

I can remember bass fishing by a beaver house and hearing a crying sound of a baby beaver. This little fellow upon seeing me slapped his teaspoon sized tail for a warning as he dove into his mother's house, and on the same day the baby loon following every move his mother would make, and thinking he was a big shot as he treadles along.

How could one forget a frosty morning looking out over a mile of marsh with the sun shimmering off all the colors and everything sparkling like diamonds?

The old stories like grandpa putting on his bottom flapped long johns in the dark and complaining to grandma that she had shrunk them only to find out he had them upside down. He looked like he was wearing shorts with long sleeves. Of course you know where his head was sticking out of. Grandma then stating "and there going to let him take a loaded gun out into the woods?"

How could I forget hooking myself in the upper thigh area and having to go to shore and pull down my pants to remove the triple hook only to find my secluded spot between two empty cabins not abandon, and then have the woman who came around the corner ask me, "what are you doing?" That one I would like to forget!

For me the memories are what hunting and fishing are all about. I would suggest that we relax and enjoy the journey and realize the moment for what it is. I will assure you if you do, those big fish or that monster buck will come your way once you realize that the memories are the real trophies.

978-0-595-40346-2
0-595-40346-8

Printed in the United States
59962LVS00004B/295

9 780595 403462